The Storybook

Collecting Your Family's Stories

Story-starters by Birdie Johnson
& Rachel Rustad
Illustrations by Char Cadra

Cover design by Jen Shaffer

ISBN 10: 1-59298-234-4
ISBN 13: 978-159298-234-9

Library of Congress Control Number: 2008926835
Printed in Canada

Beaver's Pond Press is an imprint of Beaver's Pond Group
7104 Ohms Lane, Suite 101
Edina, Minnesota, 55439-2129
www.beaverspondpress.com

Printed on recycled paper

First printing 1977
Second printing 1978
Revised 2008

Once upon a time . . .

people shared their experiences, knowledge, and heritage by telling stories. For thousands of years this delightful form of communication spread the news, taught the children, preserved the memorable occasions, and provided a large part of the entertainment for people everywhere.

In our age of technology this marvelous art has been nearly lost leaving us without the wisdom, romance, and true-life adventure: that "live" storytelling provides.

Storytelling is more than entertainment. It recounts our history as it really happened. Many of us have at least a few branches recorded on our family trees and some of us have photos of various ancestors, but very few of us are fortunate enough to know the stories behind those names and faces.

What were these ancestors like and why? How did they live and what did they think? The next time your family gathers, bring out this book. We can all enjoy reviving the art of storytelling and preserving our ancestral heritage for the generations to follow.

A few suggestions for pursuing the art of storytelling:

* Don't feel confined; just let your memory wander. Let your story amble from one event to another. Feel free to modify a story-starter to fit your unique story. Don't forget to sign and date your story, as there may be other storytellers with a different version.

* Elaborate! Tell as many of the little details as you can recall. They help to set the mood. Include pictures, clippings, or other memorabilia in the ample space provided.

* In the section marked "Bits and Pieces" you are even invited to exaggerate! After all, how do you think Paul Bunyan got so tall?

✳ *Finally, involve your audience. The give and take of ideas, the sharing of memories, and the sparkle of conversations born in a storytelling atmosphere are what make storytelling one of the most pleasurable ways of passing time.*

Blank spaces have been provided for those who wish to record the stories for a family history or for those who must share by long distance. The empty pages at the end are open invitations to write your own story-starters for tales that would fit in no one's book but your very own.

Tell your story ~ Listen to others
Share and enjoy!

Table of Contents

Spouses and Partners

On our first date together . . .

I think we have the most fun together when we . . .

Perhaps you may not even remember it, but the thing you've done for me that I appreciate the most is . . .

One of the happiest couples I've know is _____. I think it's because . . .

I need you most when . . .

The roles of men and women in our society are constantly changing. I think some of the advantages and disadvantages are . . .

I know that people change, but one quality I hope you never lose is . . .

The definition of "family" is expanding. To me, "family" means . . .

Of all the dates we had, the one I remember the most was . . .

If we had a little more time and/or money, I think it would be fun to . . .

I don't know what I would have done without you the time . . .

Every partnership has its ups and downs. The ones I can laugh about now are . . .

If I were to write the vows for a young couple committing to one another today, I think it would be important to include . . .

37

The thing that makes our house a home is . . .

As I look toward our future together,
I look forward to . . .

Parents and Children

When we first learned that you were expected, some of my thoughts and feelings were . . . and I recall with great detail that on the day you were born . . .

When you were a child, we celebrated many holidays, official and unofficial. Do you remember any of the special things we did? I remember . . .

Being a parent carries the responsibility of teaching both love and discipline to children. When I was disobedient as a child, my parents would discipline me by . . .

Some of the games I played as a child aren't played any longer. When I was little we played . . .

When you were little, I recall you liked to play . . .

Snapshots are a marvelous source of stories.
Bring me the photo album and pick out
a picture. The story behind this particular
picture is . . .

The first day of school is a memorable occasion for both parent and child. On your first day of school . . .

There is a medicine for every illness, but nothing is as good as MOTHER. When I was little and didn't feel well, my mother used to . . .

When I was young, the "latest thing" was . . .

You're one of a kind and always have been.
I remember when you . . .
And I sometimes worried about you for
various reasons. For example I . . .

There's a gradual process of changing from a child to an adult, but I suddenly felt very grown-up the time...

When children reach adulthood they begin to encounter the milestones of living. These milestones are highly emotional times for their parents. I remember how I felt when you . . .

One of my favorite things we've done as a family is ...

Grandmas and Grandpas

Progress is wonderful and it's made life much easier, but sometimes I miss the good old days when we used to . . .

Nothing matches the thrill of learning to drive or getting your first car. I remember . . .

Aside from the chores all youngsters do,
my first job for real wages was . . .

I can recall that as a child my favorite plaything was . . .

The special possessions that I hope will always stay in the family are _____ because . . .

On the day I was married . . .

Of the various animals that have been in and out of my life, I remember _____ the most because . . .

Some of our family traditions that I hope will continue to be passed along are . . .

There are many things one can do to prepare for retirement. Some of the things I think are important are . . .

If only you could have known your great-grandparents. They . . .

Fashions are continually changing and "fads" come and go. I remember when I was young we used to wear . . .

Experience is a great teacher. I think the most valuable lesson I have learned through experience is . . .

Many historical events have occurred in my lifetime: political movements, wars, scientific discoveries, natural disasters, etc. The event I recall most vividly was . . .

The president I feel did the most for this country in my lifetime was _____ because . . .

Every generation has its heroes. People from all walks of life have captured the nation's imagination. My hero/heroine when I was young was . . .

I believe the secrets of a long, satisfying, and productive life are . . .

Blessings
and
Burdens

Favors, those kindnesses given with no strings attached, create very precious memories. Many favors have been done for me but the favor most outstanding in my mind was the time . . .

I can recall many of my teachers, some by face, a few by name. But one teacher who left a truly lasting impression on my life was . . .

Teasing can be fun and most often is intended to be just that. Still, it can also be very painful, depending on one's age and the circumstance. I remember . . .

I've spent many happy moments with friends, in family gatherings, or sometimes just by myself. One happy occasion that stands out in my mind was the time . . .

We all make mistakes; many can be corrected, but there are those that must forever remain. I regret . . .

The position one holds in a family (oldest, middle, youngest, or only) affects the way one deals with life. I think my position has influenced me by . . .

The burden of making a decision that has far-reaching effects can be heavy. One of the most difficult decisions I've had to make was . . .

The best advice I ever received was . . .

Everyone has experienced moments of feeling very much alone. The time I felt the loneliest, was . . .

The five most significant incidents in my life have been . . .

Total strangers have occasionally happened through my life, each present only long enough to perform a brief kindness. They warm my heart toward all humankind. For example, I recall one time . . .

Certain events have far-reaching effects on one's life. An incident that proved to be a turning point for me was . . .

We all strive for success for ourselves and wish it for our loved ones. In my mind "success" is . . .

Being either rich or poor has its blessings and burdens. I think the advantages and disadvantages for me have been...

Hardships fall in and out of every life.
They are valuable character builders.
The hardship that I feel has affected my
character the most was . . .

Incidentals

If I could spend a day exactly as I like,
I would begin by . . .

The garment I remember most as a child was . . .

If my house was on fire and I had time to save only three possessions, I would save . . .

I once had this wild idea that I'd like to be a . . .

Mirror, mirror on the wall, if I could change one part of my reflection, I'd change . . .

I laughed the hardest the time . . .

If I could spend one hour having a chat with anyone I choose (an historical figure, someone from my family tree, a famous person) I would pick _____ because . . .

I miss the way we used to . . .

On a scale of 1 to 10, I'd rate last week (month, year) a _____ because . . .

If I could live my life in any era I choose—past, present, or future—I would choose the years from _____ to _____ because . . .

If I could go back in time and relive one day in my life, it would be . . .

Things I was sure of but now I've changed my mind about are . . .

People
and
Personalities

Our life's stories are often flavored by miscellaneous unforgettable characters. Norman Rockwell painted them, Mark Twain told stories about them. Using the following list to stimulate your memory, tell stories about your own unforgettable characters.

Boss	Chatterbox	Lazybones
Nervous Nellie	Co-worker	Perfectionist
Do-gooder	Pipe Dreamer	Enemy
Poor Sport	Friend	Roommate
Relative	Schoolmate	Know-it-all
Shy Violet	Landlord	etc., etc., etc.

And Finally ~
Share your thoughts and beliefs about the following . . .

Gratitude

Security

Milestone

Progress

Success

Change

Values

Hope

Education

Foresight vs.
  Hindsight

Loyalty

Courage

Mistakes

Charity

Failure

Purpose

Fear

Tradition

Integrity

Quality vs.
  Quantity

Violence

Faith

Economy

Ecology

Ethics

Politics

Risk-taking

Possibilities

Sticky Situations

Conformity vs.
  Non-conformity

etc., etc., etc.

And we lived happily ever after . . .

The End